# Question Time

## EXPLORE AND DISCOVER

# The Seashore

## Angela Wilkes

KINGFISHER

BOSTON

**Editor:** Carron Brown
**Designer:** John Jamieson
**DTP Coordinator:** Nicky Studdart
**Consultants:** Stephen Savage, Norah Granger
**Indexer:** Sue Lightfoot
**Production Controllers:** Jacquie Horner, Caroline Hansell
**Illustrators: Graham Allen** 18–19; **Ray Grinaway** 12–13, 14–15, 26–27, 28–29; **Alan Harris** 16*t*; **Joannah May** 4–5, 6–7, 8–9, 10–11, 20–21, 24–25; **Mike Taylor** 16–17, 22–23.
**Cartoons:** Ian Dicks
**Picture Manager:** Jane Lambert
**Picture acknowledgments: 11***tr* M. Watson/Ardea London, **15***tl* John Marsh/Ardea London; **21***tr* Keith Scholey/Planet Earth Pictures; **22***tr* Kjell Sandved/www.osf.uk.com; **27***tc* Planet Earth Pictures; **29***tl* Lorette Dorreboom/Environmental Images.

*Every effort has been made to trace the copyright holders of the photographs. The publishers apologize for any inconvenience caused.*

KINGFISHER
a Houghton Mifflin Company imprint
222 Berkeley Street
Boston, Massachusetts 02116
www.houghtonmifflinbooks.com

First published in 2001
10 9 8 7 6

6TR/0407/TIMS/RNB/128MA/F

LIBRARY OF CONGRESS
CATALOGING-IN-PUBLICATION DATA
Wilkes, Angela.
   The seashore / by Angela Wikes.—1st ed.
    p. cm.— (Question time)
   1. Seashore biology—Miscellanea—Juvenile literature. [1. Seashore biology—Miscellanea. 2. Questions and answers.] I. Title. II. Series.
QH95.7 .W53 2001
578.769'9—dc21
                                        00-047816

ISBN  0-7534-5339-8 (HC)
ISBN 0-7534-5407-6 (PB)
ISBN 978-07534-5407-7 (PB)

Printed in China

# CONTENTS

## ABOUT this book

Have you ever wondered where shells come from? Have all your questions about the seashore answered, and learn other fascinating facts on every information-packed page of this book. Words in **bold** are in the glossary on page 31.

Look and find

limpet

All through the book, you will see the **Look and find** symbol. This has the name and picture of a small object that is hidden somewhere on the page. Look carefully to see if you can find it.

Now I know . . .

★ These boxes contain quick answers to all of the questions.
★ They will help you remember all about the amazing world of the seashore.

# WHAT is a seashore?

All the land on earth—every island and continent—has ocean all around it. Where the land meets the ocean, there is a seashore. And a seashore is not like other places, because parts of it are underwater for some of the day and uncovered at other times. Seashores provide a home for all kinds of interesting plants and animals.

Red-tailed tropic bird flying out to sea to fish

Green turtles come ashore to lay their eggs in the sand every two to four years.

## That's amazing!

Oceans cover two thirds of earth's surface!

Around the arctic and Antarctica, the seashores are covered in snow and ice!

# HOW are seashores different around the world?

Seashores are different depending on whether they are in a warm or cold place, how windy it is, and what type of rocks form the land. Some seashores are just rocky ledges or tall cliffs. Some are tropical **mangrove swamps**. Others have beaches fringed with **coral reefs**. Beaches can also be sandy or covered in stones. Icy seashores are home to only a few animals, such as penguins, but many different animals can live on warmer shores.

Tide pools are found on rocky shores. They are home to many different animals, such as crabs.

# WHERE can you find animals on the seashore?

Most seashore animals hide in sheltered places. **Mollusks** and worms live on rocks or under the sand. Fish swim in the sea. Birds search for food along the shore and build their nests on cliffs. Sand dunes make a dry home for reptiles and insects.

## Now I know...

★ A seashore is where the land meets the ocean.
★ There are many different kinds of seashores around the world.
★ Animals on the seashore live in shelters that hide them.

Look and find ★ ★ edible crab

# HOW are rocky and sandy shores made?

Nothing on the seashore is ever still. Waves break, the wind blows, and the tides go in and out. The wind and the ocean make the shape of the coastline. Waves pound against the cliffs and wear them away. Pieces of rock break off. They roll around in the ocean and break up into pebbles. Then pebbles slowly break down into smaller pieces called **shingle**. In time shingle wears down into fine grains of sand.

## WHAT makes pebbles different colors?

The pebbles on a beach are pieces of many different kinds of rocks. Their varied colors show what kind of rocks they are. Sometimes pebbles are carried long distances from other coasts to be washed ashore by the ocean.

Dunlin

6

# WHY is the sea salty?

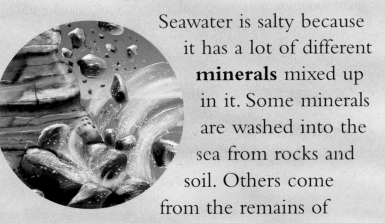

Seawater is salty because it has a lot of different **minerals** mixed up in it. Some minerals are washed into the sea from rocks and soil. Others come from the remains of plants and animals that once lived in the sea.

## That's amazing!

In some places the sand is black because it is made of lava from volcanoes!

On some seashores you can find fossils—the remains of animals that turned to stone millions of years ago!

A lighthouse is a tower with a bright light on top. The light warns ships away from rocky seashores.

## Now I know . . .

★ The wind and ocean wear away the coast, forming rocks and sand.

★ Pebbles come from different kinds and colors of rocks.

★ The mixture of minerals in seawater makes it salty.

Look and find ★ ★ cormorant

# WHY do kittiwakes nest on cliffs?

Tall cliffs and rocky islands make safe nesting places for kittiwakes and other seabirds. Here they are close to the sea and the fish they eat. But they are safely out of the reach of enemies, such as rats and raccoons. Kittiwakes crowd onto rocky ledges to build their nests of seaweed and mud. Other birds build nests with sticks or lay their eggs right on the rocks.

## That's amazing!

Guillemots lay eggs on cliff ledges only a few inches wide!

Bald eagles build the biggest bird nests!

# HOW do herring gull chicks feed?

Herring gulls catch fish, mollusks, and crabs to eat. When a parent gull returns to the nest, the chick taps the red spot on its parent's beak. This makes the parent **regurgitate** the mushy food it has just eaten, to feed the chick.

**Herring gull feeding chick**

# WHERE do puffins lay their eggs?

Puffins nest on cliff tops in the spring and summer. They dig holes in the soft grass with their large, striped beaks. Or they lay their eggs in old rabbit **burrows**, where they will be safely hidden. Puffins often stand guard near their burrows. When their eggs have hatched and the chicks have grown, the puffins fly out to sea for the winter.

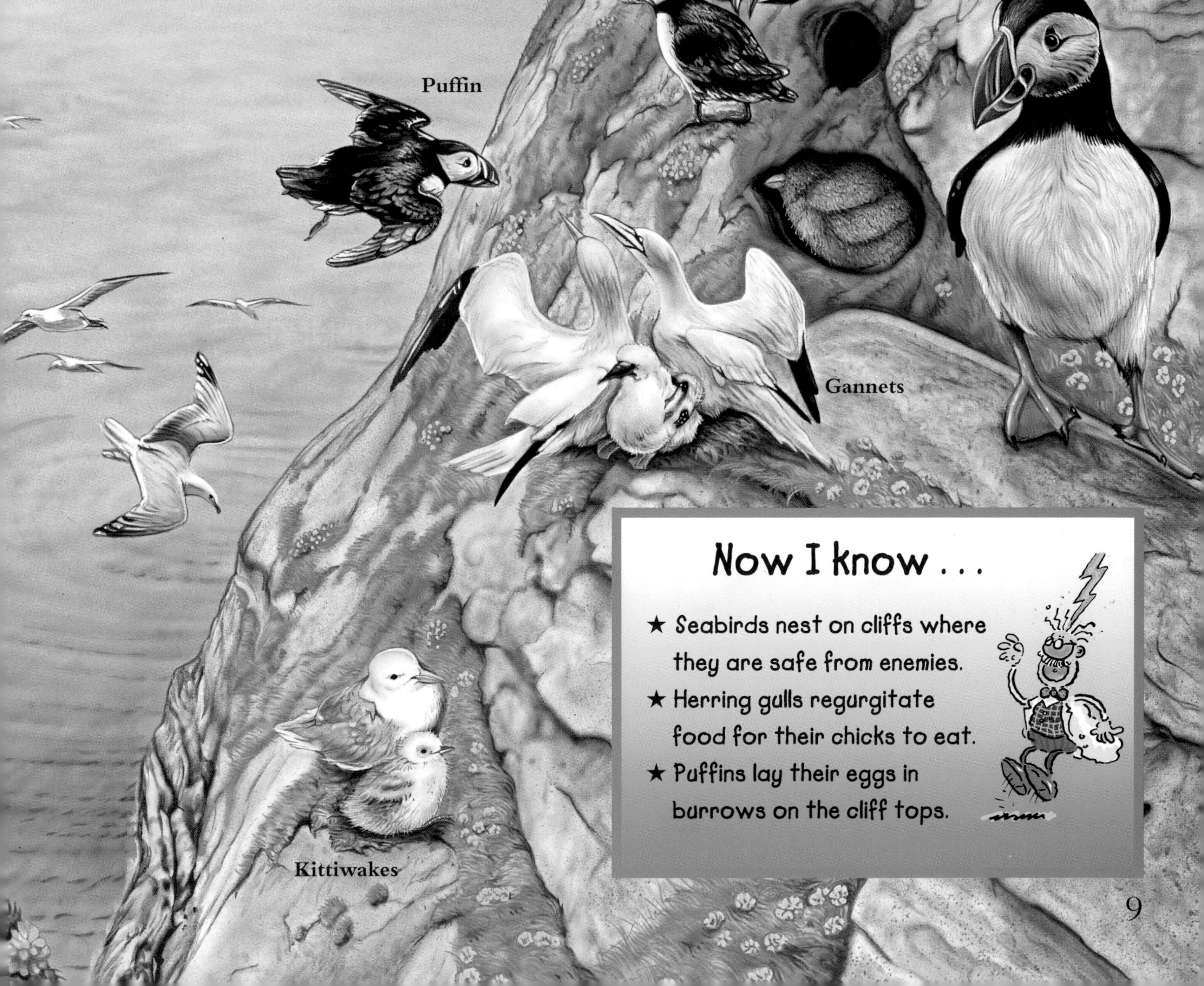

Herring gull

Puffin

Gannets

Kittiwakes

## Now I know . . .

★ Seabirds nest on cliffs where they are safe from enemies.
★ Herring gulls regurgitate food for their chicks to eat.
★ Puffins lay their eggs in burrows on the cliff tops.

9

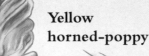

# WHAT are sand dunes?

On wide, sandy beaches, strong winds blow dry sand around. Sometimes the sand is blown toward tough grasses at the back of the beach. Then the sand begins to pile up into hills called dunes. The grasses that grow on the dunes hold the sand in place with their spreading roots. As more sand builds up, the dunes grow bigger. A thin layer of soil covers the dune, and plants grow. These attract many kinds of special animals.

**Clouded yellow butterfly**

**Yellow horned-poppy**

**Grasshopper**

# HOW do plants survive on sand dunes?

Plants on sand dunes have to be tough, because the salty breeze and sun can be strong, and there is very little water. Most plants grow close to the ground and have long, spreading roots that hold them firmly in place. Many plants have fat, waxy leaves that will not dry out or hairy leaves that trap tiny drops of water.

**Greater bird's-foot trefoil**

10

# WHICH animals live on sand dunes?

The grasses and flowers on dunes attract insects such as grasshoppers and butterflies. Lizards scuttle across the warm sand. Birds feed on insects in the daytime. Rabbits, toads, snails, and mice come out to feed at night. Foxes begin hunting for **prey** in the evening, when it is cooler. The tracks and trails of many animals can be seen across the dunes in the early morning.

Foxes and their cubs visit sand dunes in the evening to hunt for prey, such as rabbits, insects, and mice.

## That's amazing!

Marram grass grows faster if it is covered by sand!

Dunes constantly move and change shape, but plants help to slow them down!

Butterflies are attracted to the sand dunes by the colorful flowers on which they feed.

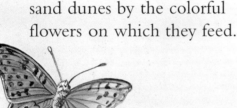

**Dark green fritillary butterfly**

**Marram grass**

**Sea milkweed**

**Silverweed**

**Natterjack toad**

## Now I know . . .

★ Dunes are hills of sand that form at the back of some beaches.
★ Plants found on dunes have long roots and leaves that do not dry out.
★ Insects, lizards, toads, rabbits, and foxes live on sand dunes.

# HOW do jellyfish get stranded?

Along the seashore the **tide** comes in twice a day, then goes out again. At every high tide, seaweed and other objects are washed up onto the shore, to be left behind as the sea goes out at low tide. A long, wiggly line of seaweed and debris across a beach shows where the high tide line is. During storms, when the sea is rough, jellyfish are sometimes thrown ashore at high tide and **stranded**.

## That's amazing!

Huge seeds from the coco-de-mer palm drift for thousands of miles!

The highest tides are at the Bay of Fundy, in Canada. They can rise over 46 feet (14 m) the height of a five-story building!

Herring gulls

Bladder wrack

12

# WHERE do shells come from?

Shells once had small animals, called mollusks, living inside of them. The hard shells protected their soft bodies. Some shells, such as whelks, are in one piece, and some have coils. Others, such as mussels, have two halves joined together by a tiny hinge.

# WHAT can you find on the high tide line?

On the beach there will be seaweed, seashells, interesting bits of **driftwood**, beach fleas, dead crabs, and starfish. You may also find the egg cases of sharks and rays and the skeletons of fish and birds. Be careful not to touch any stranded jellyfish because they can sting you.

Common starfish

Stranded jellyfish

Shark egg case

Whelks

Beach flea

## Now I know . . .

★ Sea creatures are sometimes stranded on the seashore at high tide.
★ Shells once had mollusks living inside of them.
★ You can find many different

Look and find
★ ★
limpet

# WHY do lugworms live under the sand?

It is always cool and wet under the sand, so it makes a good hiding place for animals that dig burrows. Mollusks, lugworms, and many other creatures live in burrows under the sand. There they are hidden from **predators** such as birds and crabs. The wet sand also keeps them from drying out in the wind and sun.

## HOW do burrowers eat?

Mollusks come up to feed when the tide is in. They stick tiny feeding tubes out of their shells and suck up seawater. They **filter** out bits of food, then pump out the water. Lugworms swallow sand as they burrow, eating any food they find. They squirt out the waste sand behind them, forming worm casts.

Worm cast

Sand dollar

Cockle

Pen shell

Lugworm

14

# WHERE do purple sea urchins dig their burrows?

Purple sea urchins dig their burrows in solid rock. They gnaw at the rock with their mouths and wiggle their tough spines around to scrape out a channel. They often get stuck in their burrows as they grow larger.

## That's amazing!

Razor shells can bury half of their shell in the sand in just one second!

In California, a sea urchin took 20 years to drill into a solid steel girder!

Piddock

Tellin

Razor shell

## Now I know . . .

★ Lugworms and mollusks burrow under the sand to hide.
★ Burrowers have feeding tubes that filter food from seawater.
★ Purple sea urchins dig into rocks with their mouths and spines.

# HOW do oystercatchers catch their food?

As the tide goes out, wading birds scurry along the shore, looking for food. Oystercatchers like to eat worms and mollusks, such as mussels. They use their sharp, orange beaks to pry the mollusks off the rocks. Some hammer the shells with their beaks until the shells smash. Others use their beaks to pull the shells apart and reach the juicy flesh inside.

Turnstones flick pebbles over, looking for shrimp and mollusks hiding underneath.

**Oystercatcher**

## That's amazing!

Godwits have super-sensitive beaks that can feel shrimp and mollusks moving in the sand or mud below them!

If their eggs or chicks are in danger, plovers pretend to be hurt to lure predators away from their nest!

*Look and find* **anemone**

# WHY do curlews have such long bills?

Wading birds have bills that are just the right shape for poking into soft sand or mud in search of food. A curlew has an exceptionally long bill to probe deep down into the sand, feeling for worms and mollusks. Plovers and other birds with short beaks look for food near the surface of the sand or in the water. This means different birds can feed together, but do not compete for the same food.

**Curlew**

# WHERE do plovers lay their eggs?

Plovers live on pebbly beaches and lay their eggs in shallow hollows on the ground. Their eggs are pale and speckled like the stones around them, so they are well **camouflaged**. The mother bird's feathers also match her surroundings, so enemies do not spot her as she sits on her eggs.

**Black-headed gull**

## Now I know . . .

★ An oystercatcher can open shells with its sharp beak.
★ A curlew's long bill helps it search for food in the sand.
★ A plover lays its camouflaged eggs in shallow hollows on pebbly beaches.

# WHAT lives in a tide pool?

Beneath the calm surface of a tide pool there is a busy underwater world. Seaweeds grow there, and all kinds of animals can hide and feed safely underwater when the tide is out. Shellfish and anemones cling to the rocks, crabs scuttle across the sand, and small fish dart among the rocks.

A starfish wraps its arms around a shell and pulls it open so it can eat the animal inside.

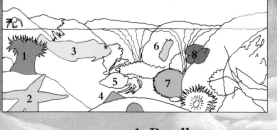

1 Beadlet anemone
2 Starfish
3 Striped blenny
4 Limpet
5 Hermit crab
6 Sea slug
7 Sea urchin
8 Mussels

# WHY do limpets cling to rocks?

Mollusks have to be able to hold on to rocks tightly or they would be smashed by strong waves. A limpet seals itself onto rocks with a strong, muscular foot, but can still move around. Mussels are attached to rocks by tough **byssus threads**. A barnacle cements itself to a rock and stays there all its life.

# HOW do sea urchins eat?

Spiny sea urchins move across rocks by gripping on with thin, tentacle-like tube feet, which suck onto rocks. Their mouths are right underneath their bodies. Sea urchins graze on seaweeds and tiny plants. They eat by scraping the plants off the rocks with their five powerful teeth.

## That's amazing!

Barnacles attract food by waving their feathery legs around!

Some sea urchins use pebbles, shells, and seaweed to disguise themselves!

## Now I know . . .

★ A tide pool is a hiding place for many different sea animals.
★ Limpets cling on to rocks for safety.
★ Sea urchins eat using their powerful, hidden teeth.

# WHY do some trees grow on stilts?

Seashores and **estuaries** in hot countries are usually swampy and fringed with mangrove trees. These strange trees can grow in saltwater. They have long roots, like stilts, that prop the trees above the mud and hold them in place. Mangrove roots stop the mud in which they grow from being washed away.

## HOW does the archerfish catch its prey?

The archerfish can shoot down prey that is out of the water. It swims up below a leaf with an insect on it and spits water at it. Taken by surprise, the insect falls into the water, and the archerfish snaps it up.

**Brown pelican**

## That's amazing!

Mudskippers can stand on their tails and jump forward 3 feet (1m) at a time!

Some mangrove trees have leaves that "sweat" salt if they grow in very salty water!

**Crocodile**

**Archerfish**

# WHICH fish can climb and skip?

Mudskippers are small fish that can survive out of water for a long time. They have strong, stumpy front fins. They use them like legs to pull themselves across wet mud and to clamber up tree roots. Mudskippers can move very fast. They skip over mud to catch their prey and hop back quickly into the water if a predator appears.

Mudskippers climb onto land to find prey, such as insects, shrimp, and worms.

**Roseate spoonbill**

## Now I know . . .

★ Mangrove trees have roots like stilts that hold them in place.
★ Archerfish squirt water at insects to knock them down.
★ Mudskippers use their front fins like legs to climb and skip.

*Look and find*

**whelk**

# WHY do crabs have claws?

Crabs use their claws to pick up food and tear it apart. They also use them to fight off attackers. Male crabs have larger claws than female crabs. Most crabs have tough shells, like armor, to protect them from predators. Despite this, they are often eaten by shorebirds, octopuses, and mammals, such as seals and otters.

This crab has its claws up, ready to defend itself from attackers.

## HOW do shrimp swim?

Shrimp have a fan-shaped tail that they spread out and use as a flipper to swim backward. They use the small, feathery legs on the back half of their bodies like paddles to swim forward. As they swim over the seabed, they pick food up using the claws on their two front legs.

**Shrimp**

# WHERE do lobsters find their food?

Lobsters find their food in shallow water near the seashore. They usually hide during the day and come out to feed at night. They are **scavengers**, eating dead or dying fish and animals. Most lobsters live near one seashore all their lives. But some lobsters **migrate** to other seashores, probably to find a new place to feed.

**Norway lobster**

## That's amazing!

Each year thousands of spiny lobsters migrate over 62 miles (100km) in single file along the seabed near the coast of Florida.

Hermit crabs do not have shells of their own. They move into empty seashells!

HOME SWEET HOME

## Now I know . . .

★ Crabs use their claws to eat and to fight off attackers.
★ Shrimp swim using their back legs and tail.
★ Lobsters are scavengers that find food in shallow water.

Look and find ★ ★ sea snail

# WHY are seaweeds slimy?

Seaweeds can be brown, green, or red. Some are flat and thin, and others look like ferns or shoelaces. Seaweeds do not have leaves or flowers. Instead they have tough, leathery fronds, like leaves. Many of them are naturally slimy, so they do not dry out in the sun when the tide goes out. Being slippery also stops them from breaking in rough seas.

## WHERE does sea lettuce grow?

Bright green seaweeds, such as sea lettuce, grow high up on the shore. Red and brown seaweeds grow farther down, near the low tide mark. Seaweeds also grow on rocks along the seashore and in tide pools. They cling to the rocks with rootlike grippers called **holdfasts**.

## That's amazing!

Seaweed is used to thicken ice cream and even to make explosives!

Giant kelp can grow 23 feet (60cm) in a day and can be as long as 196 feet (60m)!

1 Sea lettuce
2 Furbelows
3 Bladder wrack
4 Serrated wrack
5 Sea snail
6 Oarweed
7 Sugar kelp
8 Thongweed
9 Shore crab
10 Carrageen
11 Shrimp
12 Dulse

# WHICH seaweeds can you eat?

Some seaweeds are chopped and cooked like a vegetable or grated and eaten raw. A red seaweed called carrageen is used to make gelatin for jellies. Dulse, another red seaweed, is eaten as a vegetable. Some people also like to eat brown, crinkly sugar kelp and a seaweed called laver.

## Now I know . . .

★ Seaweeds are slimy, so they do not dry out and are not torn by waves.
★ Green seaweeds grow on rocks high on the seashore.
★ Some seaweeds are cooked and eaten like vegetables.

# WHICH fish live in the shallows?

Fish live in the shallow waters near the shore because there is a lot of food for them to eat there. Silvery sand eels and fish such as blennies and gobies swim just below the low tide mark. Scallops pump their way through the water. Jellyfish float around, pipefish hide in eel grass, and sea urchins and starfish creep along the seabed looking for food.

## That's amazing!

Some flatfish can change color to match the seabed!

Stonefish look like harmless pieces of coral, but their hidden spines are poisonous!

26

# WHY do flounders disguise themselves?

The flounder is a flatfish.
It lives on the seabed and lies very still.
To protect itself from enemies, it is the same color as the ground on which it lies. It flips sand over itself with its fins to complete its camouflage, so it is very hard to spot.

# HOW does a jellyfish move?

Jellyfish drift along with the tides and currents. They change direction by squeezing their bell-shaped bodies in and out. As they squeeze in, jellyfish squirt water out behind them. This pushes them through the water.

| 1 Eel grass | 5 Starfish |
|---|---|
| 2 Greater pipefish | 6 Sea urchin |
| 3 Blenny | 7 Goby |
| 4 Scallop | 8 Jellyfish |

## Now I know . . .

★ Many fish, such as blennies and gobies, live in the shallows.

★ Jellyfish drift along with the tides and currents.

★ Flounders use camouflage to hide from their enemies.

27

# WHAT is coral?

Corals are tiny animals that grow in big **colonies** in the sunny, shallow seas along tropical seashores. Many corals build stony cases to protect themselves. A coral reef is made up of many colonies and grows slowly over thousands of years. It makes a home for many colorful sea creatures.

## WHICH animals look like flowers?

Many sea anemones look like exotic flowers, with their petals swaying in the water. In fact, they are jellylike creatures related to corals and jellyfish. They live on rocks and wave their stinging **tentacles** in the water to catch their food. If shrimp or small fish brush against the tentacles, they are paralyzed by the stings and pulled into the sea anemones' mouths.

| | |
|---|---|
| 1 Sea anemone | 6 Parrot fish |
| 2 Blue starfish | 7 Butterfly fish |
| 3 Clown fish | 8 Crown-of- |
| 4 Sea fan | thorns starfish |
| 5 Giant clam | 9 Sponge |

These pieces of coral were once part of a coral reef. They were broken off to be sold to tourists.

# WHY are coral reefs in danger?

Coral reefs are being badly damaged by tourist boats and by people who break them up to use the coral as building material or sell it in tourist shops. Corals can only grow in clean, warm water. Many of them are dying as the sea becomes **polluted** with oil spills and garbage.

## That's amazing!

Clown fish have a special coat of slime so they can live safely among sea anemones!

Coral reefs grow only about half an inch (1cm) a year!

## Now I know . . .

★ Coral reefs are made from large colonies of corals.
★ Sea anemones are tiny animals that look like flowers.
★ Coral reefs are being damaged and destroyed by people.

29

# SEASHORE QUIZ

What have you remembered about the seashore? Test what you know, and see how much you have learned.

**1** How often does the tide go in and out?
a)  Once a week
b)  Once a day
c)  Twice a day

**2** Where do kittiwakes build their nests?
a)  On cliff tops
b)  On rocky ledges
c)  On sand dunes

**3** Which plants hold sand dunes in place?
a)  Seaweed
b)  Grasses
c)  Poppies

**4** Which mollusks stays in one place for life?
a)  Limpet
b)  Tellin
c)  Barnacle

**5** Which animal burrows into rocks?
a)  Purple sea urchin
b)  Lugworm
c)  Cockle

**6** Which trees can grow in salty water?
a)  Weeping willows
b)  Maple trees
c)  Mangrove trees

**7** Which animals can swim backward?
a)  Crabs
b)  Shrimp
c)  Jellyfish

**8** What object has a holdfast?
a)  Seagull
b)  Seaweed
c)  Mussel

**9** What marks the high tide line?
a)  Rocks
b)  Grass
c)  Seaweed

**10** Where do you find coral reefs?
a   In frozen seas
b)  Along tropical seashores
c)  On cliffs

Find the answers on page 32.

# GLOSSARY

**burrows** Holes or tunnels in the ground dug by animals for shelter.

**byssus threads** The tiny threads with which some mollusks attach themselves to rocks.

**camouflaged** Being colored in such a way as to blend in with the surrounding area.

**colonies** Groups of the same kind of animals living together in one place.

**coral reefs** Colonies of coral found along tropical shores.

**driftwood** Old, damaged pieces of wood carried onto the seashore by the tides.

**estuaries** Areas of water where rivers meet the ocean.

**filter** To separate food from substances such as water.

**holdfasts** The branched or disk-shaped parts at the bottom of seaweed with which it grips firmly onto rocks.

**mangrove swamps** Soft, wet, tropical coastal land covered in mangrove trees. Mangroves have long, tangled underwater roots that support their trunks above water.

**migrate** To travel from one place to another regularly, usually over long distances, to find food or to mate.

**minerals** Substances found in rocks, soil, and the remains of plants and animals.

**mollusks** Animals that have no backbones and soft bodies protected by hard shells.

**polluted** Made dirty and harmful by oil or human or industrial waste.

**predators** Animals that hunt other animals for food.

**prey** Animals that are hunted and killed by other animals.

**regurgitate** To bring up partially digested food. This is how some birds feed their young.

**scavengers** Animals that eat dead or dying fish and animals.

**shingle** Small pebbles on a seashore, usually found on the upper parts of the beach.

**stranded** Washed up and left behind on the seashore.

**tentacles** Long, flexible parts of the body that sea creatures, such as sea anemones, use to move around or to catch food.

**tide** The movement of the sea as it comes high up the seashore and goes out again twice every 24 hours.

# INDEX

**Answers to the Seashore Quiz on page 30**

★ 1 c ★ 2 b ★ 3 b ★ 4 c ★ 5 a ★ 6 c ★ 7 b ★ 8 b ★ 9 c ★ 10 b